Property Management
Best Practices

Steven M. Bragg

AccountingTools®

ISBN 978-1-64221-207-5

For more information about AccountingTools® products, visit our Web site at www.accountingtools.com.

Table of Contents

About the Author

Steven Bragg, CPA, has been the chief financial officer or controller of four companies, as well as a consulting manager at Ernst & Young. He received a master's degree in finance from Bentley College, an MBA from Babson College, and a Bachelor's degree in Economics from the University of Maine. He has been a two-time president of the Colorado Mountain Club, and is an avid alpine skier, mountain biker, and certified master diver. Mr. Bragg resides in Centennial, Colorado. He has written more than 300 books and courses, including *New Controller Guidebook*, *GAAP Guidebook*, and *Payroll Management*.

Steven maintains the accountingtools.com web site, which contains continuing professional education courses, the Accounting Best Practices podcast, and thousands of articles on accounting subjects.

Chapter 1
Introduction to Property Management

Introduction

Property owners have a large part of their assets tied up in rental real estate, and so need to employ best practices to ensure that their invested funds are used in an effective manner. In this book, we discuss how to manage tenants and ensure that a property is well maintained, while also pointing out options for increasing profitability.

What this book do not do is show you how to locate the ideal property – for that information, see the author's *Real Estate Investing* book. Instead, this book is all about the daily activities required to run a property in the most efficient and effective manner possible.

The Ideal Landlord Skill Set

The ideal landlord needs to possess skills in three general areas in order to optimize the returns on a property. These areas are as follows:

- *Property maintenance skills*. You need to have basic skills in how to clean a property, paint it, and maintain its exterior, or have access to people who can do so on your behalf.
- *People skills*. Having long-term tenants tends to reduce costs, so it is essential to have good relations with them. Therefore, the frequency and nature of your interactions with tenants will be a major driver of how quickly problems can be spotted and dealt with. Good people skills also involve seeing matters from the perspective of the tenant, which can reduce the number of areas in which conflicts can arise.
- *Management skills*. Some of the more skill-intensive tasks need to be delegated. This means knowing when to delegate, having a reliable set of contractors on call, and monitoring how well they are dealing with assigned tasks.

In addition to these skills, consider the nature of your main line of business. If you are constantly working elsewhere and so have little time to devote to property maintenance, then consider acquiring units that require minimal maintenance. Conversely, if your work situation is more flexible and you have significant repair and maintenance skills, then ownership of larger and more labor-intensive units might be an option.

Landlord Location

The initial purchase of real estate always centers on its location, but have you considered the inherent efficiencies associated with where the *landlord* is located? Proper attention to your properties will likely require many trips to them over time. Therefore, it makes sense to be situated where your daily commute or recreational routes take you past these properties. By paying attention to your own location, you can minimize excess travel time. This might even result in a landlord location just down the street from a rental unit, though doing so carries with it the potential downside of having tenants call on you at all hours of the day or night.

> **Tip:** Acquiring a small number of multi-unit properties makes more sense than a larger number of single-unit properties, from the perspective of travel time. It is just much easier to go to one location and deal with the issues of multiple tenants.

Tenant Selection

An essential property management best practice is to be picky when selecting tenants. You are looking for tenants who will respect the property (i.e., not damage it), and be more likely to stay in it for a long period of time. To find these tenants, consider taking the following steps:

- Conduct a competitive analysis against other units in the area, and develop a marketing pitch that emphasizes the key advantages of your unit.
- The best tenants prefer units that look immaculate during the initial viewing, so arrive at showings early, to clean up around the unit and dust surfaces as needed.
- Refuse to rent without a prior viewing of the property. Otherwise, tenants might have an overblown sense of what they will be renting, and so are more likely to leave at the earliest opportunity.
- Let a unit stay empty rather than leasing to a questionable tenant. Poor tenants can damage property and annoy adjacent tenants, so it is better to wait for the right tenant to come along.
- Mandate that all prospective tenants complete a rental application, on which they must list their references, criminal history (felony convictions are certainly a red flag), rental history, employment history, income, previous evictions, and bankruptcies, as well as the proposed number of occupants for the unit. Then contact their prior landlords and employers to verify this information.
- Follow up on all fields not filled out on a rental application. Applicants usually do this because they have information to hide, so it is a substantial red flag.
- A major red flag is when an applicant tries to defer the month-in-advance rental payment and/or the security deposit on your unit. This is a strong

indicator that they do not have sufficient funds to support ongoing rental obligations.

- Check state court records to see if any additional information turns up that might be relevant. This is a good place to find eviction records and felony convictions.
- Develop standard screening criteria, for which all successful applicants and cosigners must exceed a certain minimum threshold, such as a minimum credit score and income level. Establishing thresholds will eliminate those tenants least likely to renew, and which are most likely to have problems paying the rent.

Tip: One of the key indicators of a tenant who will stay with you for a long time is a history of having been steadily employed. If the reverse is the case, with a prospect revealing a great deal of job hopping, it would make more sense to wait for a more reliable applicant.

Tip: The information provided by an applicant's prior landlords is crucial. If they indicate that the person was paying rent on time, did not abuse the property, and did not generate any complaints, then you may have a winner.

Tip: Maintain records of the information you compiled when checking references. This record may come in handy if you reject an applicant, and that person then files a fair housing complaint against you.

In short, we have emphasized the need to sort through applicants to find the most reliable tenants possible. This is arguably the most significant property management best practice, since selecting the wrong applicant can lead to endless arguments and collection efforts through the term of the person's lease.

Property Profitability

You will likely pay a substantial amount for a property and plough more cash into its upkeep, against which you will be collecting rental income for many years. It is quite common for a new landlord to initially incur losses on a newly-purchased property, which means that you will need to have patience, monitoring rental prices in the surrounding area, until demand picks up enough for you to justify raising the rent. Over time, properties can reliably spin off modest amounts of cash – but it will take time to get there.

When it is time to raise the rent, there are some issues to keep in mind. For example, it can make sense to reduce the rental rate slightly in order to keep tenants for longer periods of time. By doing so, you can avoid the costs of painting and carpet cleaning that are needed when a tenant moves out, and can also avoid the lost income from periods when a unit is vacant. The following example illustrates the economics of offering slightly lower pricing to tenants.

EXAMPLE

Eric rents out an apartment for $2,000 per month in a market where he might be able to rent it out for $2,100 per month. By offering a lower rate, Eric achieves an average rental period of four years, versus an average of one year if he were to charge the market rate. By taking this approach, Eric avoids the $500 cost of turning around the apartment in each of three successive years, while also avoiding the average of one month of vacancy at each tenant turnover. The result is $96,000 of rental revenue under his current pricing strategy, versus $94,500 of rental revenue if he were to charge the market rate, minus the $1,500 cost to turn around the apartment three times.

Another consideration when setting prices is the cost of living within the surrounding area. If the costs of other essentials, such as food and health care, are unusually high, then it will be difficult to charge higher prices. In addition, periodically check the price of housing in the area, to see the average monthly mortgage rate that a tenant would have to pay in order to acquire property. This mortgage payment represents the highest amount that you can reasonably charge for a comparable rental unit, after which tenants will likely elect to buy property rather than rent.

An interesting variation on unit pricing is to offer to pay the security deposit yourself, and pay it back to the tenant at the end of the lease. Doing so is better than allowing a free month of rent, and gives the tenant an incentive to take better care of the unit, in order to eventually receive the full amount of the deposit.

> **Tip:** At the lease signing, only collect the first month's rent and the security deposit – not the last month's rent. The reason is that you might subsequently raise rental rates to an amount greater than what you already charged for the last month's rent. A court might find that the amount already paid for the last month's rent is sufficient to cover the rent – which can leave you short some rent money.

> **Tip:** Charge a security deposit amount that varies somewhat from the rate for a normal month's rent. By doing so, tenants cannot subsequently claim that the deposit was actually for the last month's rent.

When a tenant rolls over an old lease into a new one that is at a higher monthly rate, this can be a good time to require that the tenant's security deposit be increased, too. Another option that can be useful for a really long-term tenant is to offer to *lower* the amount of the deposit; this is done when you know the tenant is keeping the unit in pristine condition, and is an inducement for the tenant to keep renewing the lease.

In short, be thoughtful in setting new rental prices, and be willing to adjust your pricing requirements to appeal to the needs of your tenants.

Lease Duration

As already noted, a key driver of long-term profitability is persuading tenants to stay for a long period of time. Accordingly, it makes sense to set the lease term at one year, with occasional rentals allowed on a month-to-month basis only under special circumstances. If you allow month-to-month rentals, then that is what you will get – people who stay only for short periods of time, requiring you to refurbish the unit and advertise it again on a frequent basis.

The main scenario in which a month-to-month lease duration makes sense is when you plan to conduct a major refurbishment in the near future, and so would prefer the tenant to move out in the near term so that you can conduct the work. This option may also apply when you are contemplating selling the property, so that the buyer can decide which tenants to retain and which ones to replace. There may also be cases in which competing units are offered under monthly rental agreements, which may force you to offer the same duration in order to stay competitive.

Tip: A possible variation is to require all new tenants to sign a one-year lease, after which the lease term changes to a month-to-month arrangement. This approach provides you with more stability, along with greater flexibility to alter lease rates over the long term.

Summary

In this chapter, we have emphasized some of the key aspects of property management – selecting the right tenants and keeping them for a long period of time, while being mindful to raise rental rates when appropriate. In the next chapter, we turn to property marketing and provide more details about the tenant selection process – the first steps in property management.

Chapter 2
Property Marketing and Tenant Selection

Introduction

There are many activities required to attract the right tenants, including prepping the property, staging it, conducting cost-effective advertising, and screening applicants. We cover these topics and more in the following pages.

Identify the Target Market

Your goal is to attract great long-term tenants. To achieve that goal, you will need to determine the nature of your target market, so that you can configure the property and advertise it appropriately. To identify the right market, first look at where the property is located. If it is very close to a hospital, then the target market may be retirees who want nearby access to health care. Or, if the property abuts an elementary school, then perhaps your target market should be young couples with children. Or, as another possibility, a property near a major employer could be targeted at its employees.

Another factor to consider is the size of the unit. If it is quite small, then your market will likely be limited to singles or independent seniors. Conversely, a large unit is easily marketed at families. As another option, a unit with many amenities and large working spaces is perfect for a professional who wants to work from home. A key feature that can drive your target market is the presence of a large yard. If there is one, then it can be an attractive feature for people with pets or children.

Once you have identified your target market, all future marketing decisions will be based on how to attract those specific tenants to your property. For example, if you want to market your unit at seniors, then installing hand rails in the showers would make sense. Conversely, installing lots of storage space would be a good feature when your target market is hobbyists who need space for their side projects.

> **Tip:** If you already have good tenants in other units, ask them what they like most and least about your property. This can be useful for configuring the property to better match the needs of your target market.

Differentiating Factors

When dealing with prospective tenants, a good rule is to focus on differentiating factors that will make your property stand out from those of competing landlords. Doing so calls for an examination of competing properties, from which you can develop a matrix that compares the features of these properties. For residential properties, this matrix might address the presence of parking, square footage per unit, a pets policy, the presence of washers and dryers, and so forth.

With a completed competition matrix in hand, you can more readily identify points of differentiation. For example, you could offer a shorter lease term than anyone else, or a more convenient location, or higher-grade appliances, or perhaps just secure bicycle storage. For commercial properties, you could offer a longer free-rent period, free parking, or a larger buildout allowance. Alternatively, if you have lower overhead than the competition, then simply offer a lower-cost deal. The type of differentiation offered will depend on the type of tenant you want to attract, such as older couples, or perhaps families.

> **Tip:** When you have rental units situated within a higher-quality school district, consider making the properties more appealing to families – they will likely want to stay on the premises for an extended period of time, while their children are in school.

It is essential to have some differentiating factors, in order to attract better tenants who will be more inclined to rent from you for a longer period of time.

Prepare the Property

Much of the investigatory work of prospective tenants is conducted online, where they quickly skim through exterior and interior photos of listed properties. Since their initial evaluation is almost entirely visual, you need to focus on making a good first impression by creating a well-maintained interior and exterior, that is stocked with the amenities that local tenants want. This means reviewing competing rental properties in the neighborhood, to determine what visual elements these other properties have that your unit may be lacking. Your list of property preparation activities may be heavily influenced by what you find out during this competitive analysis. Exterior property preparation can include a broad range of upgrades, including new window screens, welcome mat, repainted door, weed removal, trimmed shrubs, and landscape lighting. Interior preparation can include faucet replacements, water line replacements (to eliminate water leaks), floor scrubbing, appliance cleaning, doorknob tightening, window treatments, paint touchups, and lighting fixture cleanings. In short, damage or dirt will turn off a prospect.

> **Tip:** When units are being shown over a period of time, check them every few days and clean again as necessary, especially when there is dust buildup or an accumulation of dead insects on the floor.

A particular concern when preparing a property is its smell. If prospects can detect any off-putting odor, they are highly unlikely to lease the unit. Several options for dealing with bad smells are to use disinfectant on the offending area, putting baking soda in the refrigerator, and dropping a whole lemon in the garbage disposal. Professional cleaning assistance will likely be needed to remove the smell of tobacco.

> **Tip:** Clean floor coverings last, after all other preparation steps have been completed. That way, anything that could possibly be dropped has already been dropped, so the resulting carpet and tile floors will remain clean until it is time to show the unit.

In short, paying attention to property preparation is a great way to attract the best tenants. If your preparation standards are low, the result will turn away the best prospects, leaving you with second-rate tenants.

Staging Issues

Showing a unit to a prospective tenant is 100% controllable. You should have sufficient time to stage the unit so that its appearance is optimal. The following tips are useful for enhancing the presentation of a unit:

- Add live flowers in the entryway and within the unit.
- Add new mulch as needed.
- Ensure that all unpleasant smells have been eliminated, perhaps via carpet replacements or repainting walls where the odors are originating.
- Illuminate any dark corners with floor lamps.
- Only show during the day, when the lighting is better (this is also a safer time of day).
- Paint the front door and the surrounding trim.
- Set the temperature to a reasonable level several hours in advance.

When possible, do not show a unit that is currently occupied, since doing so eliminates all of the presentation advantages associated with an empty unit. When a unit is occupied, you run the risk of showing it in an unclean condition, and it may contain low-quality furniture that does not show the unit in its best light. While you may think that showing an occupied unit will cut the downtime when the unit is not generating rent, you still need to prep the unit between tenants, so it is questionable whether this practice actually improves your rental income – and especially when a poor showing is turning away qualified tenants.

Advertising Options

The best way to advertise is to employ a range of options, rather than relying on a single one. Here are some possibilities:

- *"For Rent" sign.* The most economical approach to advertising is placing a "For Rent" sign in front of the property. This is most effective when there is a great deal of traffic passing in front of the property, and much less so if it is located in a cul-de-sac. A further advantage is that anyone calling you after having seen the sign has already seen the exterior of the building, and so is partway to being convinced to rent. The main downside of posting a sign is that it signals to the world that your unit is empty, which might trigger a break in.

> **Tip:** Always post a brand-new "For Rent" sign. An old, worn one subtly indicates that a property is equally old and worn.

- *Referrals.* Offer a referral fee if the referred party has paid and moved in. Or, offer an enhancement to the rental unit of the referring party, if local regulations do not allow you to make a cash payment. Local conditions will dictate the amount that you should offer. Do not delay paying the fee past the new tenant's occupancy date, since any issues after that are not the referring party's fault. This can be one of the most cost-effective ways to advertise your property.

> **Tip:** Offer an even larger referral fee during the slow times of the year, such as when you have an empty unit during Thanksgiving.

- *Flyers.* You might distribute flyers in the neighborhood and surrounding areas. This approach is good for attracting people who want to remain in the area, and they are quite inexpensive to produce. It is easy to devise a color flyer with a few key photos, floor plan, property essentials, and a map.

> **Tip:** Distribute your flyers to local employers, if they are willing to post these notices on their employee bulletin boards.

- *Bulletin boards.* Post your ads on local bulletin boards, such as in community centers and grocery stores. Leave several of the ads in each location, so that several people can take them.

> **Tip:** Indicate on the posting that the unit will only be available as of a future date, which may prevent hoodlums from attempting to break into it.

- *Craigslist.* The go-to place for rental postings is craigslist, which allows postings for free in most markets. Be sure to mention the name of the neighborhood in your ad, since most renters prefer to stay in the same area. Also include as many photos of the unit as possible, along with a floor plan, which clarifies what you are offering, and so will eliminate some prospects from contacting you.

> **Tip:** If you receive few inquiries from your Craigslist ad, keep modifying it every few days to emphasize a different aspect of the property. Also, reposting keeps your ad near the top of the Craigslist page.

- *Internet paid advertising.* There are many websites that will cheerfully place your ad for a rental unit – for a fee. It may be possible to place an ad for a reduced price on a companion website to the main site on which you are advertising. Listing the rent amount in the ad is generally a good idea, since it will automatically screen out some prospects.

- *Newspaper advertising.* Placing a rental unit ad in a newspaper has almost completely vanished as a viable option. However, if there is a local newspaper that offers reasonable pricing for its ads, then it may not hurt to try. Be aware that you may not gain many responses, since the number of readers has dropped precipitously.

> **Tip:** When you place an ad in a newspaper, read it when it is published, to ensure that there are no typos. This is a particular concern when your contact information in an ad is listed incorrectly.

If you are paying for an advertisement, include a note in the text that a prospect will receive free rent if he or she mentions this ad when calling you. The intent is to find out which advertising methods are attracting prospects, and – perhaps more importantly – which ones are not.

No matter what type of advertising you use, always advertise the property as it actually is, rather than an idealized version that does not actually exist. Doing so manages tenant expectations, rather than leaving them disappointed with the rental. The following sample advertisement presents the essentials of a property posting, where it blocks out pet owners, anyone looking for a short-term lease, and those not willing to walk up stairs. The ad also describes the location, which is useful for attracting a certain type of tenant.

> 2 BR/2 BA. $1,500/month second-floor unit in Centennial Park area for one-year lease. Pets not allowed. Rent includes utilities, all appliances are furnished. Two covered parking spots. Contact Steve at 303-123-4567 for more information.

The Initial Contact

Prospective tenants have to make a difficult decision about where to live, and that decision starts with the first impression they receive when contacting you. A good way to make a positive first impression is being easy to reach. This means that you need to return an initial contact as soon as possible. And when you do, you should be able to answer the bulk of the questions on the spot, which means having a detailed knowledge of the unit being rented. Write down any questions for which you do not have answers, and call back once you have researched them. If you are unable to take notes when talking to a prospect (such as when you are in the car), just call yourself and leave a voice mail that contains the essentials of the conversation.

> **Tip:** There is a definite sales angle to be pursued during the initial call, which is to determine what the prospect is looking for, and then sell the specific feature of the property that meets this need. For example, if the caller has young children, then you might state that your unit is a two-minute walk from the nearest elementary school.

In addition to responding to the questions posed to you, take down essential information about the caller. It is best to do so using a standard contact form, on which you note the caller's contact information and essential requirements. If the caller decides to appear for a showing, then you can continue to add information to the contact form, noting what the person liked and disliked about the unit, and whether they completed a rental application. And – always note on the form how the caller heard about your property, so that you can get a better idea of which advertising methods are the most effective.

> **Tip:** Make your cell phone number the primary point of contact. This is the best form of communication for giving prospects the information they need. It also gives you your first chance to see if the person is a credible tenant.

In order to be highly responsive to caller questions, prepare in advance a detailed listing of information about the unit, on which is stated every scrap of information that a caller is likely to ask about it. This listing should certainly include the address and square footage, and also describe parking, laundry appliances, floor coverings, and the number of bedrooms and bathrooms. Callers are also likely to ask about the neighborhood, so the listing should also cover such topics as local schools, fire stations, police stations, libraries, hospitals, grocery stores, and pharmacies.

Consider setting up a website specifically for your property, where you can post every possible bit of information about it, including photos, the floor plan, property features, neighborhood information, the rental rate, and the qualifications you are imposing for new tenants. This is quite useful, since you can direct prospects to it, rather than trying to give them the same information over the phone from memory.

> **Tip:** Buy 3D virtual tour software, and use it to create a virtual tour of your property. Then post it on the website. Anyone accessing the site can then gain a detailed view of the property.

> **Tip:** Consider creating a chart that compares the main features of your unit with other competing units in the area. That way, you can respond with favorable facts (such as your unit having covered parking or owner-paid utilities) when prospects indicate that they are reviewing competing units.

The initial contact call is not just about selling the caller on the joys of using your rental property. It is also about collecting information about the prospect, to see if the person is actually qualified to be a tenant, and whether your property would be a good fit. For example, inquiring about whether the caller has pets might immediately disqualify the person, if you do not allow pets within your property. In short, the initial call also acts as a screening tool for you, and saves you from wasting time showing the unit to someone who is not a realistic prospect.

> **Tip:** If a prospect wants to move in immediately, this can be a sign of trouble, as the person's current landlord might have just initiated eviction proceedings. In these cases, be extra careful about calling the person's prior landlords for references.

At the end of the call, ask if the person wants to see the unit. If so, set up an appointment for a specific time. Otherwise, it is quite possible that the prospect will remain in data collection mode and keep calling other landlords. At a minimum, encourage them to drive by the unit and just view it from the street. This latter approach at least maintains some level of engagement with the prospect.

Scheduling Issues for Showings

It is not efficient to keep returning to a unit for showings. Instead, consider setting aside a block of time for all showings, and then scheduling all prospective tenants in successive time blocks within that period of time. Doing so is highly efficient, and also allows you to show the unit during an optimum time of the day, when the unit presents best. As an added benefit, you can bring the unit's temperature to the optimal level for all showings, and then return it to a lower-cost setting after everyone has left. This approach will not work for commercial units, where the lease amounts are so large that it is always cost-effective to schedule in accordance with the prospective tenant's wishes.

> **Tip:** If a prospect can only view the unit during a specific time period, try to set up several other showings around that time, to maximize the use of your time.

> **Tip:** If you have to travel to the unit for a single showing, call the prospect in advance to confirm the showing. Doing so may save you a trip if the person cannot make the appointment.

An advantage of scheduling showings within a relatively narrow time block is that each party inspecting the unit sees someone else leaving when they arrive, and yet another party arriving as they leave – which makes it clear that other parties are competing to rent the property. Assuming that the unit shows well, this can expedite the receipt of completed rent applications.

A further benefit of scheduling prospects into successive time blocks is that you can give each party your full attention – which is not the case when you schedule an open house, where multiple parties may be touring the premises at the same time.

> **Tip:** Encourage prospective tenants to drive by the unit before the scheduled showing, to see if the unit has sufficient curb appeal for them. If not, you have just opened up a time slot that someone else can fill.

An alternative to individual showings is the open house, where anyone can come in during a specific time block and view the premises. This approach is useful for prospects who do not want to be the focus of any sales pressure that they think you might apply if they are one-on-one with you in a scheduled showing.

> **Tip:** Schedule an open house midday on a weekend, or late afternoon on a weekday, or both – the intent is to find a time block that will work for most of the prospects who will be interested in your property.

Sales Tips

A property rental is a large commitment of cash for any tenant, so they will want to spend some time thinking about the decision – and not feel pressured to make the decision right now. Accordingly, your ideal sales approach is a soft one, where you describe the property and the rental terms, and answer any questions they may have. Based on their questions, you may be able to enhance their interest in the unit or (equally important) disqualify the property from their consideration. The latter outcome is useful when the prospect would have been a marginal tenant or unlikely to renew the lease. In short, more listening and less talking is a good way to get the right tenant into an available property.

> **Tip:** Showing a unit means focusing on the facts – walking through every room, pointing out the parking, noting storage locations, and mentioning key nearby features that may be of interest, such as bus stops and shopping areas.

When responding to questions, your best approach is to clarify whether the unit will work for the party; if so, they will talk themselves into filling out an application. If their questions make it clear that the property would be a bad fit, then let them come to that conclusion, too. Your job is to answer their questions as honestly as possible, with no spin. They can make the decision from there.

> **Tip:** Try to fit into the conversation a question about why they want to move from their current location. Their response – such as a need for more space, or to house their 12 cats – can provide you with additional information about whether they should be renting your unit.

It can make sense to include a discussion of the property's downsides during a sales discussion. This does not have to be a lengthy list of piddling items, but rather the few items that might lead a tenant to question their decision to rent the unit. For example, they should know that railroad tracks run behind the building, and that the train will pass by at 5 a.m. each morning. This will not be a concern to someone working the graveyard shift at the local manufacturing plant, but could be a major concern for others with more traditional sleep patterns.

> **Tip:** Always have copies of the rental application on hand, in case an applicant expresses further interest in the unit. If they complete the application, check it on the spot to make sure that all fields have entries (especially their authorization for you to conduct a credit check), and that the applicant's writing is legible.

To create a modest sense of urgency among prospects, you could mention that you process rental applications in the order in which you receive them, and will offer the unit to the first person who qualifies. This statement tends to keep prospects from dithering in filling out the requisite paperwork.

A final point is in regard to those prospects that make you think they are about to sign your lease, and then point out one or two "small" issues at the last moment that would have disqualified them from consideration, such as six extra roommates or not being able to pay the security deposit just yet. There are two ways to deal with these people. One is to continually confirm their situations during the initial call and subsequent walkthrough, so that only someone intentionally misleading you would not mention a disqualifying issue. And the second approach is to be willing to walk away from the tenant, even at the last moment, and wait for a better prospect to show up. Allowing in a bad tenant is never worth the hassle, even if it initially appears that they will provide you with rent payments.

> **Tip:** To screen poor prospects, tell them during the initial call that you always conduct credit and background checks, and that you always call their previous landlords for references. This should turn away anyone with a dodgy background.

Safety Issues

A safety problem associated with showings is that you have no idea of the background of the person meeting you to view a unit, which presents the risk of assault. To minimize this concern, use the following practices:

- Only show units during daylight hours. Refuse all requests for nighttime showings.
- During the showing, have all curtains open, all lights on, and the front door unlocked.
- Depending on the situation, have a second person present.
- Obtain the full contact information for the person requesting the showing, including their phone number, name, and email address.
- Send the person a rental application and ask that it be completed prior to the showing, so that you have more information about the person.
- Cancel the showing if you have any concerns.
- Take a fake call outside, and suggest that the person view the unit alone.

Prospect Screening

Screening prospects is a major issue, since there may be any number of hidden issues that will keep you from renting a unit to someone. To minimize the risk of these hidden issues, you will need to investigate the rental history of every applicant and their credit history, as well as the sources and stability of their income. When conducting this review, be as systematic as possible, so that you don't miss any steps.

Reference checking with previous landlords is especially crucial. You should ask them about the issues that would cause you problems, such as:

- Has the person paid rent on time? If not, how late were the payments?
- Have any of the person's rent checks ever bounced?
- Has the person ever violated the terms of your lease agreement?
- Did the person give timely notice of when he or she would be moving out?
- Would you rent to this person again?

Previous landlords can provide a wealth of information about the many issues that can make a prospect a good tenant or someone you'd cheerfully evict.

> **Tip:** A gap in an applicant's rental history could indicate a period of incarceration, which you may be able to spot by running a criminal records report on the person.

> **Tip:** Consider using a tenant screening service, which provides credit, employment, and rental histories for prospective tenants.

It can be difficult to get information out of a prospect's current and former employers, other than stating their employment dates and job title. Still, this can be a good indicator of the ability of a prospect to hold a job. A string of short-term positions is a major red flag that a prospect has a difficult time earning money, and so might not be able to pay the rent.

Also, have minimum thresholds that you are not willing to break under any circumstances. For example, you may limit the number of tenants in a two-bedroom unit to five people, or exclude anyone with dogs or cats, or require positive referrals from an applicant's last two landlords. You may also exclude anyone with a criminal record. Or, you may require that an applicant have been in his or her current job for at least six months, as verified by the employer. You may also require pay stubs as evidence of a person's reported income. It is also common to mandate a minimum income level, to ensure that a prospect can afford to make timely rent payments. A good minimum threshold for income is two to three times the applicant's monthly rental payment. Finally, a common threshold is no history of having been evicted from a previous rental unit.

EXAMPLE

As a minimum standard, Joel requires that an applicant be currently employed. Henry meets this standard, as does Evan. However, Henry has been in his job as a plumber for seven years, while Evan has only been a restaurant chef for six months. If Joel's minimum standards lean toward someone with a more consistent job history, then he is more likely to view Henry more favorably than Evan. It all depends on his criteria.

You could make a formal, quantified list of criteria for a new tenant, such as 10 points for no prior evictions, five more points for a minimum income of $40,000, five more points for having worked in his or her current job for at least three years, and so forth. Under this approach, the prospect with the most points wins.

> **Tip:** Make sure that your minimum leasing thresholds comply with state and local law.

> **Tip:** Be especially careful to investigate anyone offering to pay the first month's rent and the security deposit in cash, but who has no obvious sources of income. This person is more likely to be engaged in illegal activities.

> **Tip:** If an incoming tenant has claimed that he or she is starting a new job, always call the new employer to verify that this is the case. Otherwise, you may be blindsided when a new tenant backs out of a lease before it begins.

A common approach to screening prospects is to run a credit report on the first application received, and to stop doing so as soon as you find a qualified tenant that agrees to a lease. This means that any credit report payments received from applicants for which credit reports were never pulled must be returned to the applicants.

What should you do if you have notified a prospect that they have been approved, but you are having trouble getting them to commit to renting the unit? A good approach is to set a deadline of one or two days from now, after which you will move to the next qualified prospect on your list. Delays will cost you lost rent, so do not waste time when a prospect baulks.

> **Tip:** If your screening process turns up a number of good candidates, it is possible that your rent is too low. By increasing the rent the next time around, you will hopefully match supply and demand more accurately, with just a couple of qualified candidates.

What about cases in which you have reviewed all applications and no one qualifies to lease your property because they do not exceed your minimum net income threshold? A possible option is to go back through the list of applicants and pick the one that would otherwise have been the best candidate, and ask that party if they can find a co-signer for the lease who has more financial resources.

> **Tip:** Co-signers should be located within your state. When they are located in another state, you will have to bring suit against them where they live, which will involve hiring a local attorney to handle the matter – which can be expensive.

After you have reviewed the applicants and selected one that has agreed to your lease, you will need to contact those parties whose applications have been denied. A good way is to do so using a standard notification form. This form should employ a checklist of reasons (such as insufficient employment history, insufficient income, or an adverse history at a previous rental), as well as any legally-required notifications. It is best to have a local attorney draw up this document and review it periodically, to ensure that it complies with all applicable laws.

The Lease Agreement

The lease agreement lays out the rights and responsibilities of all parties, and forms the basis for all subsequent interactions between you and the tenant. This can be a lengthy document, so the tenant might be inclined not to read it in detail, which can cause problems later. To keep this from happening, work through the document with them, summarizing each clause and having them initial the more important ones to indicate their specific agreement.

> **Tip:** To ensure that the contract is signed, never give a prospective tenant access to your property until they have signed the lease. Otherwise, tenants could claim that they have an oral agreement with you, which is then subject to interpretation.

Here are several leases clauses that can be particularly helpful:

- *Key replacement fees*. Be sure to state in the lease agreement the charges that the tenant will incur if you have to replace entry cards, keys, and/or garage door openers that you issue to them at the lease signing. Otherwise, tenants could become argumentative over why they should pay for replacements.
- *Notifications*. Make the tenant responsible for notifying you promptly when a range of issues arise within the rental unit, such as the detection of mold and dead batteries in the smoke alarms. You cannot fix what you don't know about, so this is a preventative measure to improve the safety of your property.
- *Animals*. Specify the conditions under which you allow pets within a unit, or just state that you prohibit them entirely. Either way, the tenant will have been notified about what is and is not acceptable.

Measuring Marketing Effectiveness

The costs you incur to locate qualified prospects should be measured after you have completed the search for a new tenant. This can be done with the cost per prospect calculation. Just ask each prospect contacting you how they heard about the property, and aggregate these amounts for each of the marketing methods you used. Then divide the number of prospects for each method by its cost.

EXAMPLE

David is renting a property in Smithville. He runs an Internet ad for $250, and attracts 10 prospects who mention that ad. This is a cost per prospect of $25. He also distributes flyers within the local area, hiring a neighbor to distribute them. His total cost to print and distribute the flyers is $200, from which he receives four contacts. This is a cost per prospect of $50.

These results do not necessarily mean that he should only use the Internet ad in the future, because it has a lower cost per prospect; but it should make him aware of the increased cost per prospect of using flyers.

Summary

The typical landlord does not have unlimited amounts of cash to spend on a rental unit. On the contrary, there may be barely more cash on hand than is needed to make the next mortgage payment. Accordingly, you will need to be prudent in determining your target audience, how you will contact them, and how you can be most efficient in dealing with prospective tenants who want to view your property.

Chapter 3
Tenant Relations

Introduction

Tenants are your customers, and if you provide them with good service, they are more likely to notify you of problems, provide assistance from time to time, and (hopefully) enter into extended lease arrangements. The various aspects of tenant relations are covered in the following pages.

The Key to Tenant Relations

There are many situations in which you may be required to interact with tenants, including the showing of a unit, initial screening, during maintenance issues, and while collecting rent payments. As stated previously, your profits will be higher if you can persuade tenants to stay in your property for as long as possible. Therefore, your number one consideration during these many tenant interactions is the level of respect that you show to tenants. If you deal with them in a reasonable and discrete manner, then they will be more likely to renew their lease. Conversely, if your interactions are contentious, then it is a good bet that the tenants will move on.

There are multiple ways in which you can show respect to a tenant, and encourage the other party to return the favor (thereby making your life easier). One approach is being as discrete as possible in dealing with any tenant transgressions. For example, a quiet conversation about a late rent payment is much better than posting a late notice on the person's door, where other people can see it. Another approach is to be as responsive as possible when a tenant has an issue, so that they do not think they are being ignored. If you cannot fix the issue at once, then let them know the cause of the delay, and your best estimate for when it can be remediated. For example, if a toilet leak requires a complete toilet replacement, for which you have contacted a plumber, then let the tenant know when the plumber plans to stop by. Yet another approach is electing to ignore some instances of policy breaches when they are minor, such as when a tenant's party lasts five minutes longer than the start of the official quiet time. It can be better to ignore these situations, rather than being seen as a crusty curmudgeon.

> **Tip:** If a tenant is a good one and you want him or her to renew the lease, then it pays to be more accommodating when there are modest breaches of your property policies. In short, think about the lifetime value of a tenant, rather than the annoyance of a few minor squabbles or repair bills.

Tip: It can make sense to provide new tenants with more notifications of policy violations than tenants who have been with you for a long time, on the grounds that early notifications will train the new tenants to be more respectful of the rules. After a few months, there should be far fewer policy violations to deal with.

Tip: A good way to build trust is to give tenants a gift card when they have helped you out, such as by picking up trash outside the building, or helping another tenant who was having a medical emergency.

Obviously, egregious violations, such as ongoing and very late rent payments, will require a change in your tone, since your emphasis at that point will be directed more toward replacing the tenant with a better one. At this point, a notice will likely need to be a formal written one, with the goal of an eventual eviction.

Property Rules

When developing property rules, keep in mind that a large number of restrictions can drive away the best tenants. A better approach can be to examine each policy in terms of its cost-effectiveness, to see if a tenant-friendly policy might result in higher-quality tenants. Here are examples of some property rules that might be imposed:

- *Balconies and porches.* Balconies and porches are to be kept clean at all times, with no storage allowed. Patio furniture and a barbecue are permissible. The intent is to keep the property from looking trashy.
- *Complaint times.* To preserve your sanity, require that tenants make complaints during regular business hours, unless they are having major issues. This keeps them from banging on your door in the early hours of the morning.
- *Guests.* Consider setting a limit on the number of guests within a property, and limit how long they can stay there. A few weeks is usually a reasonable limit, beyond which the added headcount can impact the wear and tear on the unit. Also, you do not want someone with a criminal record residing at the property.

Tip: Require applicants to state the car type and license plate number for any vehicles they plan to keep at the property. You can use this information to spot vehicles owned by guests.

Tip: An option is to require a long-term guest to fill out a rental application, and sign on to the lease. This can be useful, since the original tenant and the guest can now split the cost of the rent.

- *Late fees.* Establish a late fee that complies with local laws, of a sufficient size to deter tenants from making late payments. The policy should state the number of days late that will trigger the late fee. In addition, charge a daily late fee for each additional day that a payment is late. The fee should not be so large that it triggers any state usury laws. For example, the base fee might be $30, plus $5 for each additional day late. The daily charge provides an incentive for tenants to pay as soon as possible.

- *Lost key charges.* Set a charge high enough to cover your cost of keys lost by tenants, and somewhat higher to cover the administrative cost of having the keys replicated. You might consider charging a higher fee when a tenant is locked out after your normal operating hours.
- *Minimum temperature.* State the minimum temperature at which the thermostat must be set, so that the pipes don't freeze in cold conditions. This can be an important issue when tenants want to save money by turning off the heat while they are away on vacation.
- *On-site businesses.* You might require prior approval before tenants start up any businesses from within their rental units. This can be a major issue, with more tenants electing to work from home.
- *Painting.* It can make sense to prohibit the repainting of units by tenants, since this can result in drips and spills that will eventually need to be cleaned up. Another option is to allow modest repainting by longer-term tenants, if only to improve relations with them. Also, if you decide to allow painting, consider setting a requirement that only neutral paint colors be used, so that you can continue to use the same color after they have moved out.

Tip: If you allow a tenant to paint a room, then take a picture of the paint can, so that you will have the color and sheen information that will be needed to touch it up at a later date.

- *Parking.* Each tenant is assigned a numbered parking spot, and overflow guest parking is permitted in any unnumbered parking spots. Those parking in the incorrect spot may be towed. This is an especially important rule if you are charging tenants for reserved parking spots.
- *Pets.* Many landlords prohibit pets, on the grounds that it may be necessary to replace the carpeting after a tenant moves out – or, at a minimum, that the carpeting must be subjected to a deep clean. Insurance premiums may also increase if you allow pets (usually due to claims associated with dog bites). If you elect to allow pets, then be aware of the additional maintenance costs associated with them. At a minimum, allow pets on approval, which allows you to forbid the keeping of dangerous pets or those that are not housetrained.

Tip: If you have a unit for which the carpeting is approaching the end of its useful life, consider offering it to prospective tenants who have pets. They will not have to worry about damage to the carpet, since you will be planning to replace it once they eventually move out.

> **Tip:** As part of your reference checking for an applicant, ask prior landlords if there were problems with the tenant's pets. This information can be useful for denying an applicant whose pets have a history of being troublesome.

- *Potted plants.* Tenants may want to keep potted plants within their units. If so, leakage can result in damage to the property, so consider imposing a rule for where plants can be kept. Ideally, plants should only be allowed in areas where moisture cannot cause stains, such as on concrete patios. Also, consider imposing a rule to ban potted plants from locations where they can fall onto passersby, such as railings.
- *Quiet times.* If you are renting out a condo unit or part of a townhouse, it may be necessary to impose a quiet period. This is needed to avoid complaints from neighbors who might have issues with your tenants making too much noise late in the night.
- *Security deposits.* A security deposit is needed to cover any damage caused by a tenant. The amount of this deposit is usually set at one month's rent, or somewhere close to that amount[1]. Your policy should state how long you will hold the deposit, what deductions you can take from it[2], whether you will pay interest on it, and whether an additional deposit will be required if the tenant chooses to keep a pet on the premises.

> **Tip:** Conduct a survey of competing properties, to see what size deposit they require. This is a competitive issue, so you may want to set the same deposit level as the competition, or somewhat lower.

> **Tip:** If you allow a new tenant to pay for a security deposit over several months, do so under the agreement that subsequent payments from the tenant will be directed first to the deposit and second to lease payments. This approach increases the size of the deposit more quickly.

> **Tip:** Talk to new tenants up-front about the circumstances under which you will deduct from their security deposits, so there are no hard feelings at the end of the lease term, when you take deductions. The discussion should cover what they can do to avoid any deductions. To strengthen your position, take a video of the unit before the new tenant moves in, so that you'll have visual evidence of its condition.

---

[1] The amount of a security deposit may be capped by state law.
[2] Allowable deductions from a security deposit vary by state, but generally include unpaid rent, cleaning, unreturned keys and remotes, and damages to the extent that they exceed normal wear and tear.

EXAMPLE

Myrna cannot make deductions from a tenant's security deposit for normal wear and tear on her property, but it is allowable to deduct a percentage of the replacement cost if the tenant has caused damage that exceeds the normal amount of wear and tear. In the current situation, a tenant has caused an irreparable acid burn on a wall hanging. The hanging is four years old, and would normally be expected to have a ten-year life. Since the wall hanging cannot be fixed, Myrna will have to spend $500 to replace it. She would be justified in deducting $300 from the tenant's security deposit, which represents compensation for the six years' remaining life that has been lost.

Tip: Return deposits by certified mail, so there is no question that you paid back the funds.

- *Smoking.* Many landlords prohibit smoking within their units, on the grounds that it can be difficult to remove the associated odor. This is a particular concern, because many prospective tenants will not rent a unit that contains any trace of tobacco smoke.
- *Sub-letting.* Some tenants may want to sub-lease their space, especially if they have had to move elsewhere prior to the end of their lease, and need to generate some income from the unit. The policy should state that sub-letting is subject to your approval, so that you can keep questionable tenants from moving into the property.

Generally, it can make sense to impose property rules only under certain conditions. For example, rather than excluding pets entirely, you could state that only one pet is allowed per unit, or that dogs under 30 pounds are allowed. Similarly, rather than prohibiting car washing in the parking lot, consider allowing it only on weekends.

Tip: Keep the policy list fairly short, so that it fits onto one sheet of paper, and post it in each unit. That way, tenants might actually read it.

Consider having your attorney review the list of property rules, to ensure that they comply with state and local regulations. The attorney should be particularly focused on tightening up the language to ensure that they cannot be misinterpreted.

Once you have finalized the rules, have your tenants sign the document at move-in, acknowledging that they will abide by the rules. This sign-off makes the rules legally binding.

Tip: If a particular problem keeps coming up that is not covered by the rules, it may be a good idea to include a new rule pertaining to the issue. However, keep in mind that an excessively long list can be a turn-off for tenants, and may even persuade them to move elsewhere once their lease expires.

Tenant Onboarding

A good way to make a positive first impression with a new tenant is to offer them a welcome package, such as a free pizza coupon with the local pizzeria, or perhaps a bottle of wine. Conversely, it may not make sense to offer a few hours of free maintenance at the start of the lease, since this might give them the impression that you will always provide such services for free.

New tenants have a bad habit of calling with questions, which may result in you having to repeatedly stop by the property to settle various issues. A more efficient use of your time is to be *extremely* thorough in walking through a unit with the tenant once they have signed the lease agreement, discussing every possible issue at that time. Topics to cover may include policies, where the trash and recycling are kept on trash day, how to deal with common maintenance issues, how to maintain appliances, how to use the fire extinguisher, how to access the mail, and so forth. In essence, you are investing more time up-front in order to avoid additional issues down the road.

Tip: Keep a list of tenant issues, which may give you clues for how to improve your onboarding process. If certain issues keep coming up, then you should include them in the onboarding discussion.

Tip: Maintain a binder that contains printouts of all appliance user manuals, for tenants to use. Doing so minimizes the risk of tenants damaging appliances due to misuse.

A good way to save time with tenant issues at the end of a lease is to walk through the unit at the beginning of the lease, mutually writing down the condition of each item. This review should include everything, including the condition of doors, windows, storage, lighting fixtures, appliances, air conditioning, and so forth. Both parties sign and keep a copy of the resulting document, which is later used to evaluate the condition of the unit when the tenant eventually moves out. This best practice is a good way to avoid arguments when you find a problem at the end of a lease term that will result in a deduction from the tenant's deposit.

Another good onboarding activity is to provide each new tenant with a move-in letter. This letter provides them with useful information that they will need during the first few weeks of their tenancy, such as how to set up utilities in their name, sign up for trash removal, contact the local school for child enrollment, and so forth. Not only is this information highly useful to the tenants, but it also keeps them from badgering you with questions about these items.

Tip: Confirm that new tenants have switched the utilities billing to their name before you hand over the keys. Otherwise, you will be responsible for paying the utility bill.

Develop a tenant handbook for each unit that provides answers to most of the questions that a tenant is likely to ask about, such as the phone number for the local fire station, or when rent is due, or which parking space is allotted to the unit. The intent behind providing this handbook is to minimize the times that tenants call you, so structure the handbook with that goal in mind.

> **Tip:** Post a QR code in a prominent place in the unit, with instructions to scan it in order to access an online version of the tenant handbook.

Tenant Training

To reduce maintenance costs, consider setting up an information sheet next to items that are most likely to trigger a tenant complaint (such as a clogged toilet). Doing so may eliminate some complaints entirely. Another option is to walk tenants through the simpler repair activities, noting where the related tools are located on the premises. Again, the intent is to apply a modest amount of tenant training in order to reduce calls.

It can also be useful to walk tenants through a few basic repair prevention activities, such as not banging into the hoses underneath a sink. It can also be useful to discuss how closet doors function, and how to get them back onto the support rails.

If you allow tenants to paint their units, a useful training topic is to describe to them the need for drop clothes and painter's tape. It may even make sense to issue them drop clothes and tape, since doing so can reduce the number of drips that will otherwise need to be cleaned up.

Tenant Assistance

Local laws may limit your access to a rental property, so it will be necessary to enlist the aid of tenants in spotting repair problems and reporting them to you. This is essential, both for spotting small problems before they become big ones, and also because prompt fixes are more likely to result in happier tenants. You can ask tenants to report issues to you, and also make this request in a formal move-in letter. When making these requests, point out the specific issues you want to hear about, such as rodents, water damage, appliance problems, and clogged gutters.

Collecting Rent from Tenants

Collecting the full amount of your rent payment on time, every time starts with the initial tenant selection. If you spend the time researching the financial circumstances of each applicant, it is vastly more likely that they will pay you with great regularity. The next action needed to ensure timely payments is a consistently applied rent payment policy. This policy states when rent payments are due, where it is due, and what happens if a tenant's payments are late. Consider including in the policy a requirement that all payments made after the grace period must be made with a money order or cashier's check – which eliminates the risk of having a late payment also bounce.

Tip: If your tenants pay by sending you a check in the mail, make the process easier by providing them with a set of stamped self-addressed envelopes that cover the entire term of their lease.

Tip: You can set the rent payment to coincide with the receipt of cash by a tenant. For example, set the rent payment date to be shortly after tenants receive their monthly social security payments, disability payments, or rental payments.

In addition, consider using any or all of the following options to remind tenants to make rent payments on a timely basis:

- Remind them via a text message or an email
- Send them a monthly invoice
- Call them during normal daylight hours to remind them when a payment is late
- Call upon them at their unit, to remind them of the amount of any late payments

A good way to put a positive spin on rent payments, if you own a number of units, is to hold a monthly prize drawing, such as a gift certificate, for all tenants who have paid their rent on time. Be sure to notify everyone of the winner, since doing so reminds the tenants of the positive effects of paying on time.

Direct personal contact is almost always the best way to obtain a late rent payment. If this contact results in a workout arrangement, document it and have the tenant sign it; otherwise, it will be of no use in court.

Tip: Establish a late payment fee that is high enough to incentivize tenants to pay on time, without being unreasonable. Consider imposing it as a daily fee, so that (for example) a tenant who pays five days late will owe a late fee of $50, assuming that the fee is $10 per day.

Tip: If you charge a late fee, do not waive it. A waiver sends the message that it is acceptable to make late payments, since there is no downside to doing so.

From an efficiency perspective, a good payment policy is to require just one payment from each rented unit, rather than from each tenant within that unit. This reduces your payment tracking, forcing this task onto the tenants, who must collectively pool their funds to make the payment. This approach also puts the burden on the tenants to ensure that each one of them pays up on time.

Tenant Payment Options

The traditional approach to accepting payment from tenants is by check, but a better option is to set up auto-pay, so that you can extract the monthly payment directly from their bank accounts. Another option is Venmo, where tenants can make an online payment, avoiding the need for any paper-based payments. Auto-pay is an especially appealing option, since it eliminates the risk of late payments. You can even include the auto-pay requirement in the lease agreement, which may eliminate some prospective tenants from consideration.

> **Tip:** If you must accept check payments, then provide tenants with self-addressed stamped envelopes for the entire term of their leases. Doing so gives them one less reason not to pay you on time, and you can use the postmark date on the envelope to determine whether payments have been made late.

> **Tip:** Charge tenants the bank's fee for any bounced checks, which gives them an incentive to ensure that they have sufficient funds in their checking accounts to cover all check payments.

You could impose a policy that any bounced checks will immediately trigger a requirement that all subsequent payments be made with a money order or cashier's check. Another option for a perennial late payer is to come to a mutual agreement that the tenant's lease should be terminated early, perhaps in exchange for not charging any damages against the individual's security deposit. That way, you can begin the search for a more reliable tenant, while the current tenant has the opportunity to look elsewhere for less-expensive housing. A further advantage for the tenant is that there will be no eviction notice on his or her credit record.

Changing the Rent

Your goal is always to keep the best tenants for the longest period of time. With that goal in mind, how should you go about raising the rent? To avoid losing the best tenants, only change the rent at relatively long intervals, such as once a year (typically at the point when a lease is up for renewal). However, do not wait too long to make a rental increase, such as once every two years, because then you may be forced to make quite a large increase in the rent, which could be a turnoff for tenants.

Another technique for retaining these tenants is to keep your rental rate slightly below the market rate, on the grounds that it is much less costly for a tenant to absorb any rent increase than to pay for a move to a new location.

Tenants are more likely to accept a rent increase if you accompany the change with a moderate enhancement to the property. For example, you might replace the carpeting, or swap out the oven for a more efficient one.

Tenant Communications

You will receive comments from tenants all the time, asking for various things, such as whether they can have a ninth cat on the premises, or allow a friend to live as their guest on-site for a few months, or perhaps to park a sailboat in their driveway. While some of these requests will be unique, most will be repeated over time by various tenants. In the latter case, consider devising the best possible response and recording it in a binder. You can then memorize these standardized answers and trot them out whenever subjected to them by a tenant. Taking this approach makes it easier to make decisions, and allows you to deal with tenants in a more consistent manner.

Regular status updates may be appreciated by tenants. Posting updates to a website for the property is nonintrusive, but tenants may not check it regularly, especially those without Internet expertise. An option that works well for all ages of tenant is a simple newsletter, posted in a common area. This newsletter can provide information about (for example) seasonal maintenance reminders, when the parking lot needs to be cleared for maintenance, and changes to the departure time for the shuttle to the local shopping center.

> **Tip:** Most communications should be in person, since it is all too easy to convey the wrong impression through a poorly-worded printed message or email.

Dealing with Broken Leases

There will be times when a tenant has to move out of a unit before the final date of the lease, perhaps due to a job change, a divorce, or an ill family member. In this situation, tenant rights laws in many states mandate that you have to make a reasonable effort to re-rent the unit, and can only charge the departing tenant for any actual costs incurred to market the unit, as well as any unpaid rent until the replacement tenant starts to pay rent. In this situation, a good tenant relations technique is to get the tenant on your side in re-renting the unit as soon as possible. This can be done by pointing out that you are within your rights to continue deducting rent from the tenant's lease deposit while you are trying to find a new tenant. The departing tenant can reduce the amount of this deduction by moving out as quickly as possible and leaving the unit in pristine condition. That way, you can advertise it again at once, hopefully resulting in a quicker move-in for the replacement tenant. In short, try to get the departing tenant on your side when a lease is broken.

> **Tip:** Document your effort to re-rent the unit associated with a broken lease (including a printout of the posted advertisement), in case the prior tenant disputes the amount of the rent deduction from his or her deposit. Also document all deductions for expenditures related to repairing the unit during turnaround.

Dealing with Difficult Tenants

Some issues with tenants cannot be resolved. They may continually break your after-hours noise policy, argue with neighbors, keep prohibited pets, and so forth. While some landlords will put up with this behavior and just wait for a tenant's lease term to expire, you should consider the interim negative impact on your other tenants. It is entirely possible that you will lose these tenants in the meantime, because they cannot put up with the stress of dealing with the annoying party. In short, by allowing a tenant to continually engage in bad behavior, you are losing the opportunity to retain other tenants over the long term, which impacts your profits. Consequently, a better approach is as follows:

1. Issue enough warnings to determine whether the tenant's behavior can be fixed.
2. If not, begin proceedings to evict the tenant as soon as possible.

> **Tip:** You might not realize that a tenant is causing problems, unless you maintain routine and cordial relations with your other tenants in the area – which is another reason to keep up the communications.

Assume that any tenant problem could eventually lead to that party's eviction. That being the case, it makes sense to document every infraction. Doing so gives you a historical record of tenant problems, which is excellent proof in case the situation eventually ends up in court. In particular, always issue a written notice that each successive late payment is grounds for eviction. Even if you do not immediately go through with an eviction, this paper trail of notice will support your case for eventually doing so.

Evictions can be both expensive and traumatic. Consider an easier alternative, which is to allow a tenant to voluntarily move out without paying any further rent, or any rent that is currently unpaid. Doing so may be less expensive than an eviction.

Tenant Lease Extensions

It is frequently useful to have tenants extend their leases – as long as they are good tenants. If that is the case, then you can avoid a substantial amount of unit turnaround costs and advertising fees by encouraging a lease extension. Here are several best practices to encourage tenants to stay:

*   Start the lease renewal discussion several months in advance, before the tenant is actively looking for other places to stay.
*   Provide superior service at all times, so that repair and maintenance issues will never be a reason for a tenant to leave.
*   Ask the best tenants in advance if there is anything you can do to improve their units.
*   Unilaterally provide unit upgrades, such as a new kitchen countertop or ceiling fans (especially useful when the rental market is weak).
*   If tenants are having some financial difficulty, offer them a month-to-month lease, so that you can evaluate their circumstances in a few months, when they may be in a better position to commit to a longer-term lease.
*   Offer a professional carpet cleaning to start off their renewal period.
*   Offer a few hours of free maintenance labor for whatever they want done to their unit.

> **Tip:** If a current tenant wants *a lot* of upgrades before renewing, consider a modest rent increase that covers the cost of the upgrades.

In addition, consider altering the termination date of your lease renewals, so that they end during the high season, when demand is strongest. By doing so, you will no longer run the risk of having an empty unit right at the time of year when tenant demand is at its weakest.

Tenant Departures

Tenants tend to be much less careful when they are moving out of a unit than when they originally moved into it. They are also likely to stuff trash receptables with unwanted items, and may even leave a fair amount of furniture in the unit. And while doing this, their helpers may take up excess parking space and annoy the neighbors. To minimize these actions, a good best practice is to issue a move-out letter, in which you state how the tenant is supposed to check out, and also what you expect from a final walkthrough of the unit (in regard to its condition). The letter should note the types of deductions you will take from their deposit, noting specific types of damage that will trigger a deduction. When tenants have been given notice that they will lose money if a departure does not go well, they are likely to be much more careful.

> **Tip:** The move-out letter should be quite detailed, noting exactly what should be cleaned within the unit, where to put trash, and to give you their forwarding address, so you will know where to send the residual amount of their deposit. Also, note the locations of nearby donation centers, which can reduce the amount of trash left with the unit.

> **Tip:** Look in on the unit during the move-out process, to get an idea of whether the departing tenant will actually be out on time. You will need this information to schedule the turnaround process for the unit.

Conduct your final move-out inspection of the unit only after the departing tenant has removed all items from it. Otherwise, there is a chance that the tenant was using some strategically-placed items of furniture to mask damage to the floors and walls.

It can make a great deal of sense to return the full amount of a deposit to a tenant, unless there are serious damages for which you require restitution. In other cases, tenants might take you to small claims court, which will chew up more time than any deposit deduction might have been worth.

> **Tip:** If you do elect to make deductions from a deposit, be sure to provide the former tenant with an itemization of the deduction. These deductions should be defensible in court, so only deduct actual amounts expended, for which you have receipts. A high level of detail reduces the risk of a tenant challenge to the deduction.

Tip: If a departing tenant was a good one, ask them if you can provide them with a letter of recommendation for their next landlord. They may be so surprised by this that they will be extra careful in moving out, leaving you with fewer repairs to deal with during the unit turnaround process.

Summary

In general, try to view all situations from the viewpoint of the tenant, try to make their living arrangements as easy as possible, and take every opportunity to make casual conversation with them. This tenant-forward approach is a great way to ease relations with tenants over extended periods of time.

Chapter 4
Repair and Maintenance Issues

Introduction

A rental unit can become a money pit, unless you are careful about what types of repairs and maintenance to make, how they are prioritized, and whether a variety of best practices can be applied to this function. We address these issues in the following pages.

Prioritize Activities

There are always more repair and maintenance issues than you can realistically deal with in the short-term – especially when your budget restricts the amount that can be spent. Consequently, make a formal, prioritized list for each property, where tenant safety issues are always dealt with first. After that, invest in preventive maintenance, since doing so protects the long-term value of the property. Finally, consider upgrades that can increase the rental rates charged; these items are typically installed after a tenant has moved out, and so can be scheduled for discrete points in time.

In addition to the items just noted, it is also important to deal promptly with issues that might otherwise cause an exodus of tenants. For example, if the roof leaks and this is a major problem for the applicable tenant, then assign a higher priority to this fix. By focusing on repair activities from the perspective of the tenant, you can increase the odds of keeping tenants for a longer period of time.

> **Tip:** Be aware of the minimum housing standards set by your local government. If your property falls below these standards, tenants may legally have the right to withhold rent payments, or sue for damages.

Standardize to Save on Maintenance

You might waste money maintaining stocks of repair items, because you have not standardized on the features of each unit. For example, painting all units the same color means that you only have to stock one color of paint to do touch-up work on all of them. Similarly, installing the same brand of LED lights in all units allows you to maintain a smaller number of LED replacement lights. The concept also reduces complexity from the perspective of product knowledge. For example, installing the exact same type of garbage disposal in every kitchen of your residential units makes it more efficient for you to repair and replace them, since you only have to know how to deal with one type of disposal. Another possibility is to use the same carpeting on all of your units and then lay in a stock of excess carpet, which can be used to patch or replace carpet everywhere.

Tip: It is best to avoid high-end appliances and flooring, since they are expensive to install and maintain. Also, when a high-end appliance dies, the tenant might insist that you replace it with a comparable unit. Instead, use mid-range appliances and flooring.

Tip: It is easier to standardize when you acquire a multi-unit property, since it was likely constructed using the same fixtures.

Another possibility is to lay in a stock of parts for appliances, such as the knobs on stoves and ovens for which replacement parts are available. Doing so saves time when you want to replace one of these items on short notice during a turnaround. This concept works best when you have the same appliances in all units, so the stock of parts can be used in all of your properties.

Conduct Preventive Maintenance

It is highly cost-effective to conduct preventive maintenance, where you spend a small amount on a recurring basis to avoid larger repair bills down the road. When conducted properly, preventive maintenance can also extend the life of some elements of your property. For example, an annual review of the air conditioning unit can identify worn-out parts and optimize how it functions, thereby also reducing tenant complaints during the warmest part of the year. Or, you could swap out the entire inside of every toilet in your units on a scheduled basis, which reduces the cost of excess water from running toilets.

A particular advantage of preventive maintenance is that you can conduct it whenever you want to do it, versus having to repair worn-out or broken equipment in the middle of night, which seems to be when so many maintenance issues arise. The result is lower overtime charges from anyone you are paying to deal with these issues.

Tip: Schedule contractors to perform preventive maintenance during their slow seasons. They may charge lower prices at these times, and will certainly be easier to schedule than during their busy seasons.

Go Green

As you update units over time, consider going green. This means installing tankless water heaters, heat pumps, weatherproofing, water-reduction fixtures, double-pane windows, and energy-efficient appliances. When installed prudently, these investments will save money over time. In addition, you can advertise these enhancements when advertising for new tenants; these upgrades will tend to attract more energy-conscious and responsible tenants.

Avoid Furnishings

It is generally not a good idea to furnish a unit. Furnishings are expensive, and require maintenance or outright replacement at regular intervals. Further, you may lose some prospective tenants who already own their own furniture. And furthermore, it is better to have a unit completely cleaned out between tenants, so that you can more easily conduct maintenance on it.

The only case in which it can make sense to furnish a unit is when your target market expects it – such as students at the local university. Also, there may be a few cases in which there is an expectation within the local market for units to be furnished.

Minimize High-Maintenance Items

Certain items can attract renters, but are so expensive to maintain that they are not worth installing. In particular, hot tubs, saunas, and pools can require so much ongoing repair work that they should be avoided. If you have acquired a property that contains these items, it can make sense to rip them out.

Tip: Go over the insurance on a property with your insurance agent, to see if the insurance can be reduced if certain installations on the property are removed.

High maintenance also applies to flooring. An expensive wood floor may require more frequent replacement, as may lighter-colored carpeting. This means limiting your flooring choices to alternatives that are durable and hide stains easily.

Another high-maintenance item is large trees, and especially when they are located adjacent to the property. Trees drop leaves and branches, which need to be cleaned up, and also clog the gutters.

Another concern is larger parking lots, especially when there is more parking space than is required by tenants. These lots need to be plowed in winter and will also require refurbishment from time to time. Therefore, where possible, try to match the available parking to tenant requirements.

Another item to watch out for is entryways that do not have paved access. If tenants have to cross gravel or dirt before they can access the building, then gravel or dirt will be tracked into the building, which wears out the flooring at a rapid rate. Consequently, a good preventive maintenance action is to pave the access points to the building.

An easy preventive maintenance fix is to ensure that downspouts drain water well away from the structure. When this is not the case, standing water adjacent to the structure can, over time, damage its foundation.

Conduct One-Call Fixes

In some cases, it can be more effective to conduct a somewhat more comprehensive fix in a single visit than to make a quick fix and then be called back multiple times to make additional repairs. The classic case of this situation is a leaking or non-operable toilet. Though it may initially be less expensive to replace a single part within the toilet mechanism, it is almost always more efficient over the long term to replace the entire set of toilet tank components, thereby eliminating the majority of toilet problems with one fix.

Conduct Repair-or-Replace Analysis

A key consideration is whether to repair or replace an appliance. There are a few indicators that can assist in making this decision. If the repair is relatively minor, such as a seal replacement or the replacement of a minor part, then a repair is likely to be warranted. However, a major component replacement (such as a motor) is likely to be so expensive that it will make more sense to replace the appliance. The latter decision is even more likely when the appliance is nearing the end of its useful life.

> **Tip:** Replace water heaters early, rather than late. Doing so minimizes the risk that they will leak, and potentially cause extensive damage.

For some appliances, the cost of almost any repair is prohibitive, making it easier to swap out the old appliance for a new one. This is particularly the case for microwaves and refrigerators.

When you elect to replace an appliance, review whether certain features are more likely to break or cause problems (such as ice cube dispensers on refrigerators). When this is the case, it can make sense to downgrade to a more basic unit that does not contain the problematic feature.

> **Tip:** The repair-or-replace analysis is more likely to tip toward replacements when you are planning to sell the property in the near future. If so, this is a good time to install significant upgrades that can increase the selling price of the property.

Upgrade the Paint

A paint application may last for a number of years, if you invest in the best possible paint. In particular, buy semi-gloss paint for the high-impact kitchen and bath areas. Having semi-gloss paint makes it easier to clean up stains, and it is also more resistant to moisture.

> **Tip:** Always clean the walls before applying any paint. In addition, deal with all grease stains, water stains, and so forth before applying the paint. In particular, deal with the sources of water stains before painting a surface.

Protect the Unit During Repairs

It is all too easy to damage a unit or cause stains while you are in the process of maintaining a unit. For example, dragging in a new water heater can damage the floor, while paint from a touch-up job can end up on the floor. To minimize the risk of these events, have tarps on hand for all maintenance work, and spread them wherever there is the slightest risk of damage. For example, they should be spread over furniture while conducting ceiling repairs, and on the floor when wheeling or dragging anything into or out of the unit. They can even be spread over the lawn when you are replacing roof tiles, in order to catch nails.

Provide Tenants with Maintenance Tools

Some tenants may be interested in conducting their own maintenance, which eliminates the time and cost of doing so yourself. To encourage this behavior, maintain a stock of the more essential maintenance tools on-site, where tenants can access them. For example, leaving a few snow shovels on-site encourages tenants to clear snow from the driveway and walkways, which has the added benefit of reducing the risk of liability from falls on the premises.

Outsource Selected Activities

Some activities will need to be outsourced, especially when they require either special skills, special equipment, or timely interventions. For example, it is quite common to outsource snow removal to a business that has adequate snow plows, as well as a proven track record of being able to clear driveways and walkways within a few hours of the most recent snow storm. Similarly, it makes sense to standardize with the same HVAC provider for all of your units, since this provider will then have a good knowledge of the heating and air conditioning units at your properties, and will be able to service them more quickly than other parties who are called in without a detailed knowledge of the situation.

> **Tip:** Specialized activities that should usually be turned over to a contractor include plumbing, electrical, roofing, HVAC, concrete work, remodels, and reflooring jobs.

If you are personally located a long ways away from your rental property, it will be exceedingly difficult to oversee it yourself. A better option is to hand over the property to a professional property management company. This advice also applies if you are not skilled with maintenance activities, or find that you have a difficult time standing up to the demands of your tenants. Other advantages to using a property management company are as follows:

- They can advertise, screen prospective tenants, and show the unit to prospects
- They have more expertise to deal with a broad array of property maintenance issues
- They are staffed to deal with after-hours emergencies
- They collect the rent for you
- They can enforce property rules

> **Tip:** If you want to be somewhat involved in the management of your property, you can arrange to pay a reduced amount to a management company in exchange for a reduce level of service.

Tip: Only hire a property management company that solely manages property. Real estate offices also offer property management services, but they are not solely focused on this activity, and so tend to provide worse service.

Tip: Verify that the management company you select carries insurance for general liability, professional liability, automobile liability, and workers' compensation. Otherwise, you may find that a failure by the company could result in claims against you.

Tip: Require your management company to store your cash transactions in a separate bank account. If they are commingled in a common account with the transactions of the company's other clients, you may have a hard time getting your money back if the company goes bankrupt.

These significant advantages must be balanced against the associated property manager fee. Property managers may also charge a significant markup on any maintenance work conducted[3]. A further concern is that property managers may not put forth their best effort to fill vacancies in your units, since they may also be managing a large number of other units for other clients at the same time.

Tip: Look for a property management company that charges a percentage of the collected income on your unit. This approach gives them an incentive to maximize the unit's rental income.

Tip: Do not enter into a long-term property management agreement, since you may want to fire a manager that is not doing a good job for you. If the manager insists on a long-term arrangement, include an early-termination fee in the agreement, so that you have to pay a modest amount if you elect to terminate the company.

It is especially useful to shift all legal activities to a qualified attorney, since attorneys with experience in the real estate field can keep you out of court, saving you more money than they cost.

Assess at Turnaround

Whenever a tenant vacates a unit, this is the ideal time to conduct a thorough assessment and identify preventive maintenance issues. By blocking out the time to assess a unit and conduct thorough repairs, you can substantially increase the life of the unit, while also keeping it in good shape for new tenants.

---

[3] Some property managers charge a low property management fee and then charge above the market rate for repairs and maintenance. They can use this strategy to turn an especially large profit on older properties.

While preventive maintenance during the turnaround period is always a good idea, this does not mean that you should renovate to an excessive degree. Instead, just ensure that your units have the standard features possessed by all competing units in the area, and ensure that they are maintained at a competitive level. Otherwise, over-renovating just means that your incremental rent gains from making these adjustments will likely be lower than the incremental cost of making them. Ideally, the typical unit should be in reasonable condition, which means clean and functional.

> **Tip:** Look at the ceiling for water damage. If you see a stain, there is a good chance that there is a water leak occurring in the unit above the one you are inspecting.

Repurpose Specialized Areas

Unless there is a clear cost-benefit case to be made for a specialized area within a unit, it is generally not worthwhile to retain it. For example, an exercise room or media room can be expensive to install, and yet provides little return in the form of increased rent.

Manage Rebillings

There will be times when a tenant caused damage that you are repairing. When this happens, you will need to keep track of the cost of the repairs, since these costs will be rebilled to the tenant. You may need this recordkeeping for those cases in which a tenant protests a repair and refuses to pay it.

Summary

Once you have found the right tenant through a proper screening process, the next great impact on your profits will be the repairs and maintenance function. Astute management of this activity can be the difference between a consistent money loser and a valuable property that generates consistent positive cash flow.

Chapter 5
Additional Profit Opportunities

Introduction

A rental property may not be overly profitable, so it always makes sense to seek out new sources of revenue, especially those with few offsetting costs. In this chapter, we cover a number of additional revenue options, as well as possible ways to reduce expenses.

Additional Leasable Space Revenue

There may be an opportunity to rent space on the premises that is currently not being rented at all. For example, if you are using on-site storage space for your own requirements, could it make sense to move out your storage items and reconfigure the space as rentable tenant storage space? Similarly, if you have several parking spots reserved for your own use, consider eliminating one or more of them and converting them into reserved tenant parking – for a fee. This item will not represent a large revenue increase, but it does maximize your use of space.

Furnishings Revenue

If your target market happens to be renters who want a furnished unit, then you can charge extra for the furnishings. This situation is most likely to be the case for short-term renters, such as when a local employer uses your property to house out-of-town employees who might only be on the premises for a month or two. These situations tend to comprise a small minority of all rental situations, but if that is your market, then a (not insubstantial) investment in furnishings could pay off handsomely.

> **Tip:** There are businesses that will provide you with a complete set of furnishings, but this rental cost will severely reduce your incremental income from providing fully furnished units.

Internet Revenue

Many tenants work from home, and so will appreciate fast Internet access, with large upload and download speeds. If you pay for fiber or cable Internet access to your property, tenants will likely be willing to pay a modest monthly fee for access to this connection. There will be a cap on what you can charge, since tenants have other options – such as satellite Internet and digital subscriber lines.

Laundry Revenue

Depending on the nature of your property, a good choice is to add a washer and dryer to each unit, and increase the monthly rent to offset this capital cost. Tenants will use a substantial amount of electricity when running the washer and dryer, so be sure to have the tenants pay for all utilities.

If you are operating an apartment complex, you could build out a laundry facility, to be used by all tenants. This may involve investing in your own washers and dryers, or you can have a laundry-service contractor bring in its own machines and service them for you. In the latter case, the contractor sends you ongoing payments for your share of the proceeds. Though the contractor will take some of your profits, you will not have to make the initial capital investment, and there will be no machine maintenance to deal with.

> **Tip:** Use a cashless payment system, to avoid damage to the machines from vandals who want to steal money.

Parking Revenue

If your property is located in an area where parking spots are in short supply, then consider charging for reserved parking spots. Better yet, if the local weather conditions are harsh, consider building covered parking or garages for tenants. In the latter case, this will require an extra investment to construct the necessary structures.

> **Tip:** Separate your rent charges into unit rent and parking rent. Those tenants who do not own vehicles will appreciate the reduction in rent.

Unfortunately, charging for parking will require some additional rules for tenants. You will need to issue parking stickers for all reserved spots, and install signage for reserved parking spots. In addition, separate keys will be needed if you rent out garages. You will also need to contract with a local towing company to tow away cars incorrectly left in reserved parking spots.

Private Rentals Revenue

If your property has significant clubroom or pool facilities, consider renting them out for private functions. If so, ensure that your insurance will cover any possible claims that might arise from such usage. Of course, private rentals will only be available for larger properties, so this is generally not an option.

Purchase Option Revenue

Some tenants might be interested in purchasing your property at a later date. If so, you can offer them a purchase option in addition to their rental agreement, where the amount of the option is a credit toward the eventual purchase price that they pay for the property. Under this arrangement, the tenant will have the option at the end of the lease term to purchase your property at what you and the tenant jointly agree will be the market value of the property at that time. When the tenant's lease expires, he or she may elect to deduct the amount paid for the option from the market price of the property, and you can immediately sell it. Or, the tenant does not have the cash to close the deal or does not close for some other reason, and so loses the purchase right, along with the amount paid for the option. In either scenario, you win – either by selling the property at market value or by recording the amount of the purchase option as revenue. Of course, this is only a viable option if you are willing to sell the property.

> **Tip:** An added benefit of the purchase option is that tenants are quite unlikely to damage the property while they are in it – after all, they might end up owning it in the near future.

Your main downside to using the purchase option is that the market value of your property might unexpectedly go up by a substantial amount during the lease term, in which case the tenant buys the property at the pre-agreed price, and you lose out on the extra gain in value of the property. You can guard against this downside by keeping the duration of the purchase option relatively short, such as one year.

> **Tip:** Another way to guard against the loss of appreciated value in your property is to include a clause in the purchase option that increases the tenant's purchase price by the average price increase in the neighborhood during the term of the option.

There can be negative tax consequences associated with purchase options, so have a real estate attorney draft the document for you.

Storage Revenue

Tenants might greatly appreciate the option of renting extra storage space. This might take the form of weatherproof, exterior storage units that can be locked by the tenant. These should be solidly constructed, so the initial capital cost could be relatively high. Nonetheless, quality construction translates into longer-term viability, so these units are likely to require less maintenance over the long term. A further advantage is that having storage units on the premises that are available to rent will entice tenants to move their other off-site storage into these units, because they are close at-hand. In addition, they will tend to remove clutter from the rental units, making your property more visually pleasing to the casual visitor (such as a prospective tenant).

Forms of Indirect Revenue

There are several situations in which you can increase the available group of tenants who might be interested in your property, which are based on changes in your operating policies, as well as some modifications to your rental units. With higher demand comes an opportunity to raise your rental rates, and therefore your profits. These best practices are noted in the following bullet points.

- *Allow pets.* As noted elsewhere in this book, you can increase the interest in your property if you allow pets. This will require a change to your policies, and will likely need some strict boundaries around what types of pets will be allowed. This approach will only work for certain properties in which you expect to swap out the carpeting soon anyways, or where there are old wood floors that cannot become even more scratched. If you have a fenced yard, this is also a good draw for pet owners.

> **Tip:** Require pet owners to pay a larger security deposit. After all, you might need it to repair the damage caused by their pets.

- *Allow college lease durations.* Landlords tend not to like renting to college students, because they default on their one-year leases as soon as the school year ends. A different approach is to charge more per month, but to offer leases that only span the normal nine-month school year. That way, you maximize your revenues, while the students do not need to default on the lease.

> **Tip:** Require student tenants to post a larger security deposit, since this group is more likely to cause damage to rental property.

- *Upgrade facilities for senior housing.* As the population shifts in an older direction, there is substantial demand for senior housing. Seniors can be excellent tenants, since they are generally quieter than the norm, cause less damage, and are more likely to renew their leases. Upgrading your facilities to accommodate senior needs should be based on an analysis of whether your property's location meets the needs of seniors, such as ready access to shopping, entertainment facilities, and hospitals.

Expense Reduction Opportunities

There are several areas in which you might achieve noticeable reductions in the expenses associated with a rental property. In the following bullet points, we note several opportunities:

- *Appeal property tax assessments.* It can be worthwhile to appeal your property tax assessment, possibly every year. You are more likely to achieve a reduction in the assessment during a recession, when property values are declining.
- *Bid out insurance.* Put your property insurance out to bid every few years, to see if any insurers are willing to offer a lower price. In addition, review your existing coverage to see if there are any instances of over (or under) insurance.

Another option is to discuss with your insurance agent whether any property improvements could reduce your insurance premiums.

- *Bid services.* While there are benefits from maintaining relations with the same service providers for many years, it can still be worthwhile to bid out this work from time to time, to see if you can get a better deal.
- *Shift utilities to tenants.* Install unit-level utility metering within your property, so that individual tenants can be billed for their own utility usage.
- *Reduce utility usage.* As the cost of utilities increase, it makes even more sense to reduce utility usage. Possible steps to take include setting up an ongoing maintenance program for your heating and air conditioning systems, switching to newer and more efficient heating and air conditioning systems, and installing more insulation in the building.

Summary

In addition to providing you with extra revenue and profits, the added services noted in this chapter also provide real benefits to your tenants, and so can be useful for attracting new ones.

Chapter 6
Organizational Issues

Introduction

There are lots of activities associated with property rentals, and staying organized ensures that they are all completed as efficiently as possible. In this chapter, we cover the general organizational structure of your filing system, as well as the need for checklists, calendars, budgets, financial statements, and similar items.

General Organization

It helps to be as organized as possible, to improve the efficiency of your daily tasks. Here are several organizational tips:

- *Tenant files.* Maintain a separate file for each tenant, in which is stored a tenant's rental application, credit report, reference information, lease agreement, move-in checklist, and any other written communications. This file should be updated throughout the duration of a lease, including records of rent increases, maintenance requests, repairs made, and correspondence with the tenant. Archive these files once a tenant moves out, in case there are subsequent lawsuits or some other landlord calls with a request for referral information about one of your prior tenants. At a minimum, keep these files for four years past a tenant's move-out date.

Tip: If you allow pets in a rental unit, consider photographing them and keeping these photos in the applicable tenant files. This is useful for when you are trying to determine whether a pet has been replaced, or which of the pets owned by your multiple tenants has caused damage.

Tip: All lease agreements should be in writing. If you enter into a verbal agreement and there is a dispute later about those terms, you will likely lose in court. Courts tend to favor tenants in these situations.

- *Lease renewal dates.* Keep close track of each tenant's lease renewal date, so that you can contact them in advance about extending their lease.
- *Postmarked envelopes.* If a tenant sends you a rent payment by mail that is late, keep the envelope on file, so that you have proof that the enclosed check was mailed late. Similarly, keep the envelope when a mailed security deposit is returned as being undeliverable; the envelope provides proof that you tried to return the money.

- *Unit files.* Maintain a history of the repair and maintenance operations conducted on each of your units, and especially on items that require periodic updates, such as furnace filters and carbon monoxide sensor batteries. This information is useful for scheduling recurring maintenance.
- *Receipts and expenditures.* Maintain a formal recordkeeping system, so that cash receipts and expenditures are stored by accounting period, where they can be easily accessed. If there are several properties, then these records should be maintained separately for each property.
- *Warranties file.* Most appliances come with a warranty. If so, store them in a file, along with a note identifying the unit in which each appliance is located. It may also make sense to maintain a master record of all appliances, noting when they were purchased, where they were installed, and any repairs made to them. This summary form is useful for estimating when you may need to budget for appliance replacements.
- *Insurance file.* Store your insurance policies in a file, and maintain a summary page on which is stated the name of the insurer, the type of policy, what is covered, and each policy's expiration date. Also maintain in the file a record of all insurance claims made, and correspondence to and from the claims adjustor.
- *Service contracts file.* Store all third-party service contracts in one file, so that you can readily access the relevant contractual details. This is especially useful for ensuring that billed amounts match what was specified in the contract.
- *Ownership file.* All documents associated with your ownership of a rental property should be included in an ownership file, which is stored in a fireproof container. This should include your deed[4], due diligence inspection reports, environmental reports, pest control reports, and any related correspondence.
- *Maintenance supplies and equipment.* Centralize all maintenance supplies and equipment, with each item stored in a designated location and properly labeled. Doing so makes it easier to discern whether any items are missing or need to be replenished. Examples of the items that can be included in central storage are paint brushes, putty knives, wrenches, screwdrivers, shovels, brooms, nails, screws, caulk, bleach, and cleaning solution. It can make sense to store similar items together, such as paint brushes, rollers, painter's tape, and paint.

Tip: Keep more expensive and fragile items, such as carbon monoxide sensors and light bulbs, in a higher location in storage where they are less likely to be damaged by other supplies and equipment.

Tip: Monitor the types of batteries required by your smoke detectors and carbon dioxide sensors, and keep a supply of them on hand.

---

[4] An even better storage location for a property deed is a safety-deposit box at the local bank.

Tip: It can make sense to maintain stores of certain items within or adjacent to rental units, such as ladders, shovels, brooms, and any supplies used on a regular basis. Doing so is especially useful for items that are difficult to transport from a central storage location.

- *Paint and stain identification.* Properly identify all paints and stains, including a label on each one that identifies the unit in which it was used.

Some of the information that we have recommended keeping in the preceding bullet points includes lots of private information about your tenants, so keep these files locked up, so that intruders cannot access it.

Checklists

A few checklists can be useful for property management. Of these, the most important is the move-in checklist, on which you document the condition of the unit and any furnishings provided to the new tenant. This is quite useful later, when the tenant moves out and you need to assess any damage caused by the tenant (which is deducted from the associated security deposit). This is also a good way to identify which of the furnishing belong to you, in case the tenant later disputes their ownership.

Tip: Have tenants jointly go over the move-in checklist with you, and have them sign the document when the review is complete. Better yet, have tenants fill out this form in their own handwriting. This gives you a good basis for making deductions from their security deposit later, if there is damage to the unit.

Tip: Have tenants complete the move-in checklist before they move anything into the unit, since there is a good chance they will cause damage to the unit during the move-in process.

Tip: If you make any subsequent repairs to a unit, such as replacing a plumbing fixture, alter the move-in checklist to reflect this change, and have the tenant initial the adjustment.

Another checklist itemizes the items to review following a tenant move-out, to ensure that you have found all issues that need to be fixed before the next tenant can move in. This list can be extensive, including an examination of ceilings, doors, windows, bathrooms, counters, appliances, and even an odor check. These activities can include running all appliances, to ensure that they work properly. The checklist should also include battery swaps for all smoke detectors and carbon monoxide sensors, as well as a routine changing of the locks.

> **Tip:** Keep a copy of the repairs checklist in a unit that is being turned around, so that you can easily update it as tasks are checked off and new ones are found.

Another checklist is a listing of the tools and supplies that will be needed for unit turnaround activities. This checklist will rarely be complete on the first pass, so keep it posted in a prominent place for a few days, and update the list as you think of any additional activities that need to be completed.

Perhaps the most critical of all, prepare a checklist that shows exactly how to shut off the utilities – which is handy in case there is a fire, flooding, or other disaster. This checklist should include a floor plan that points out exactly where each shutoff point is located, and a procedure for how to safely conduct the shutdown. The procedure should also note which tools are needed to complete a shutoff. The phone number for the local utility company should also be included at the top of the procedure, where it is hard to miss.

The Due Diligence Checklist

Of particular interest to the buyer of a property is the due diligence checklist. When contemplating a purchase, you should systematically go through a detailed listing of every possible issue, to see if there are any concerns that would keep you from purchasing the property. Here are some of the more critical items to include on the checklist:

- Do any rent controls apply to the property?
- Do any tenants have expectations for work that was not done by the current owner?
- Does the current owner have bank records for all security deposits?
- Has an inspector provided a list of all repair and maintenance issues?
- Has the building been inspected to ensure that it matches local building codes?
- Has the current owner provided a complete file on each tenant, including a history of payments, background checks, credit screenings, maintenance requests, legal notices, and complaints?
- Has the current owner provided a complete repair history for each unit?
- Has the current owner provided copies of all service contracts associated with the property?
- Has the current owner provided copies of the latest utility bills?
- Is there a complete list of all personal property that will be included in the sale? This should include photos and serial numbers.
- What is included in the insurance policies carried by the current owner? A copy of the loss history under the policy is a good way to learn about damage issues related to the property.

Maintain a Calendar of Activities

Some property maintenance issues should be completed on a regular schedule, such as swapping out furnace filters and the batteries in carbon monoxide sensors, or cleaning the gutters. Given the regularity of these activities, it makes sense to set up a calendar of activities, with specific actions required on certain days. Depending on where your properties are clustered, it may make even more sense to complete the same tasks for all units on the same calendar day. Other activities should be conducted at longer intervals, such as a monthly or quarterly inspection of the exterior of the building.

Another possibility is scheduling regular checks by professional exterminators. It is better to keep pest levels as low as possible, rather than having their presence drive tenants away.

> **Tip:** Include an energy audit on your calendar, to have someone review your units and recommend changes that can reduce energy usage.

> **Tip:** Schedule maintenance at your properties near the end of the month, which makes you visible to tenants a day or two before their rent is due. This reminds them to send you a payment, and may result in them handing it to you on the spot.

Maintain a Listing of Actions Taken

Consider maintaining a listing of every action taken for each unit, when the actions were taken, and how much they cost. This is useful for communicating back to tenants who might otherwise complain that you are not dealing with their complaints in a prompt manner. It is also useful for tracking the history of maintenance actions taken, so you can plan for the next date on which recurring maintenance steps will be necessary.

Maintain a Contractors List

Contractors will be more responsive if you keep using the same ones over time, since you will then represent a larger proportion of their sales. To ensure that this is the case, maintain a go-to list of contractors, and use it. Better yet, list primary and secondary phone numbers for each contractor, as well as a weekend contact number. By having multiple options for contacting a contractor, you will stand a better chance of getting a response in the event of an emergency.

Maintain a Comparable Properties List

There are likely to be a number of properties around town that are comparable your own in terms of their square footage, appliances, amenities, local services, and so forth. Develop a list of these properties and occasionally research the rental rates being charged for them. This information is quite useful for setting the rental rates on your own units. Also, researching the same competing properties over time provides you with good information about the direction in which rental rates are trending.

> **Tip:** When updating your listing of rents on comparable properties, try to take into account all discounts that the other landlords are offering. They may actually give you this information, once their units have been rented.

To calculate the net monthly rent on a competing unit, divide the total amount that a renter would pay by the number of periods in the lease. Thus, if a unit is advertised at $2,000 per month for a two-year lease with the first two months free, then the net monthly rent will be $1,833 (calculated as 22 months × $2,000, divided by 24 months).

Prepare Income Statements

To understand how well your rental units are performing, be sure to create a separate income statement for each one. This statement should address all expenditures on separate line items, so that you can clearly see where cash is being spent. This means having line items for mortgage payments, electricity, water, homeowners' association fees, lawn maintenance, trash pickup, legal fees, management charges, and repairs and maintenance. It is especially important to trace repair and maintenance costs to specific units, so that you can more easily see if a unit is persistently generating losses.

Prepare a Capital Expenditure Schedule

It is helpful to conduct a periodic review of all capital expenditure items associated with a property, such as the roof, parking lot, cabinets, appliances, windows, air conditioning, and boiler. Then include the estimated replacement dates for these items in a CapEx schedule, along with the estimated date on which replacement will be required. With this information in hand, you can easily budget for a cash reserve in each year, that gradually increases until it is sufficient to undertake the necessary asset replacement. For example, if a roof has a remaining useful life of 20 years and will cost $40,000 to replace, then you can budget for an annual set-aside of $2,000, which will have grown to the required amount by the time the roof is ready for replacement 20 years from now.

> **Tip:** Consider the side effects of waiting too long to replace an asset. For example, not replacing a roof for a few years past its normal replacement date will delay a cash outflow, but may cause structural damage due to leaks.

Prepare a Budget

At the beginning of each year, prepare a budget for each unit that is based on your historical rental revenue and expense performance. Then adjust the budget based on your plans for the next year, such as a rent increase (or decrease), changes in the repair schedule, and any expected payments for capital expenditures (as discussed in the preceding section). In addition, consider adjusting budgeted revenues for changes in market rental rates, expected rental discounts, property tax changes announced by the local government, and expected turnaround times when you are between tenants. The resulting budget represents your best view of cash inflows and outflows, and so can be used to estimate your cash flow for the next year.

> **Tip:** If you have just purchased a property for a price significantly higher than what the previous owner paid for it, there is a good chance that its value will be reassessed by the local government to your purchase price, which will increase your property taxes.

> **Tip:** If you are planning to buy a condominium, review the financial statements of the governing association. If it is not building a reserve for future major repairs, there is a good chance that you will eventually be whacked with a major special assessment.

Identify Cost-Benefit Issues

Proper organization of property management activities includes a formal analysis of which costs should be incurred, based on the return generated. And more importantly, this analysis should identify which costs are to be avoided. In the following bullet points, we note those activities having the highest cost-benefit, and which should therefore be scheduled for completion as soon as possible:

- *Painting*. Paint is relatively inexpensive, gives excellent surface protection, and provides a notable cosmetic improvement to any property. This means that painting needs to be one of your first improvement activities in all parts of a property, both on the inside and the outside, and extending to patios and fences. Always use high-quality paint, since it lasts longer and requires fewer applications.
- *Caulking*. Caulk is inexpensive, and protects against water damage both inside and outside of a unit. It can also be used to fill in smaller cracks in concrete and asphalt surfaces.
- *Dryer duct cleaning*. Lint can build up in dryer vents, which can become the source of a fire. Schedule periodic checks to clear out all lint from these vents.
- *Mats*. Mats can be strategically placed in high-traffic areas throughout a unit, thereby reducing wear on the underlying carpet or hardwood floor. This is especially important at the front door and garage door, where a doormat traps dirt being carried in on visitor shoes from the outside. Large area rugs can also be used to protect flooring elsewhere in the unit; these are good investments, as long as they are relatively inexpensive.
- *Monitoring systems*. Invest in smart water monitors and shutoffs for every unit. These devices can identify water leaks, shut off the flow of water, and send you an alert through a smart phone app. Though these units are moderately expensive, they can reduce your water bills due to leaks, and can prevent catastrophic water damage to a unit.
- *Ventilation*. Proper ventilation is needed to minimize moisture buildup within a unit, which can cause mold to form. Therefore, ensure that bath and kitchen fans are working properly, so that moisture is being correctly vented to the

outside. This means cleaning dirt from the fans and ensuring that the exhaust outlet has not been blocked. When fans are not working properly, replace them.

Other expenditures that are relatively inexpensive, and which can significantly enhance the visual impact of a unit, are for replacements of outdated lighting fixtures, ceiling fans, and electrical switches, as well as kitchen cabinet refinishing.

> **Tip:** Concentrate your paint purchases with a single paint specialty store, since it will keep your paint color codes on file. In addition, on-staff specialists can make recommendations about which paints to use.

> **Tip:** Invest in bath fans that automatically turn on when the bathroom light is turned on. Doing so ensures that the moisture generated by showers and baths is automatically vented out of the unit.

As a general rule, any investment is a reasonable one if you can expect to be fully paid back within a period of two years, assuming full unit occupancy during that time.

EXAMPLE

You have been renting out a property for the past decade, and the current tenant has notified you that she is moving out. The current monthly rent is $2,500. An inspection reveals that the property's exterior and interior are in need of a major refresh, which will cost $80,000 and also require you to keep the premises vacant for three months, while the required work is completed. Upon completion, you should be able to increase the rent by an additional $1,500 per month, which is $18,000 per year.

In short, the cost is $7,500 of lost rent while the property is being renovated, but it would likely have been unoccupied for at least one month if you had elected to instead undertake a modest touch-up instead, so the cost of not renting the unit is probably closer to $5,000. When added to the $80,000 remodeling cost, the total cost is projected to be $85,000, against which you can offset $1,500 per month of additional rent. This results in a payback period of 57 months, or nearly five years. Whether that is a good investment is up to you, though an additional consideration is whether you might eventually need to lower the rent in order to attract tenants, in the absence of a refresh.

Track Tenant Issues

An important organizational issue is to maintain a log of tenant contacts, when you received them, when you settled them, and (most importantly) which ones are still outstanding. This log is useful for tracking your performance in assisting tenants, as well as in monitoring outstanding issues. Without a log, there is a good chance that tenant issues will fester, possibly resulting in a higher rate of tenant turnover than you would like.

Tip: Another way to enhance tenant relations is to ask them to fill out a form once a year, in which they itemize any issues they are having with the property. This is a useful way to catch problems before they become major concerns, and also to enhance relations by quickly responding to the issues they point out.

Monitor Turnaround Time

One of the most critical issues for any landlord is the duration of the period between tenants. No rent is being paid during this period, so close monitoring of the turnaround time is needed to keep cash flows in a healthy state. This monitoring can have a secondary effect, which is an increased emphasis on using contractors to conduct repair and maintenance tasks. Contractors can be extremely useful for shortening turnaround time when you don't have enough in-house staff to complete all planned repair and maintenance activities within a sufficiently short period of time.

Tip: Contractors are especially useful when you have to turn around multiple units at the same time. In this case, it is more important to re-rent the units right away, rather than waiting a few months while you personally update each unit. In short, the cost of contractors is much less than the revenues generated by immediately being able to rent the units.

Turnaround time tracking can also be applied to tenant complaints, and can result in the same emphasis on using contractors. If you want to maintain healthy relations with tenants, the quickest way to deal with their concerns may very well be to bring in contractors when your own staff is overwhelmed with work requests.

Obtain Insurance

It is essential to obtain landlord's insurance that provides specific types of coverage. Consider whether you will need the following types of coverage within this policy:

- *Structural replacement.* Will the policy pay for a complete replacement of the structure if it were to be destroyed? If so, will it provide full replacement value for the property?
- *Wrongful eviction coverage.* Will the policy provide protection against claims arising from a wrongful eviction?
- *Premises liability.* Will the policy pay the legal and medical bills in the event of an accident occurring on the premises?
- *Property manager coverage.* Will the policy extend its coverage to actions taken by your property manager?
- *Lost rental income coverage.* Will the policy pay you the amount of lost rental income while the property is being rebuilt or repaired?
- *Sewer backup coverage.* Will the policy pay for damage to the premises that is caused by clogged sewers?

The basic package offered by most insurers does not cover damage due to falling objects, glass breakage, water damage from plumbing failures, or damage from the weight of snow or ice. Coverage for these items is included in broad-form coverage, so be sure to obtain that type of insurance. An even higher level of coverage (for a substantial price increase) is special-form coverage, which covers all possible losses unless they are specifically excluded.

In addition, consider obtaining an umbrella insurance policy that provides coverage for claims exceeding what is covered by your underlying insurance. Please note that this policy will require that you maintain adequate amounts of base-level insurance before it will start to provide coverage. These policies are usually inexpensive, and can provide substantial additional coverage.

What will not be covered by these standard policy types is damage due to earthquake or flood damage. For this coverage, you will have to pay extra. It can be useful to explore whether a property you are planning to purchase is located in a flood plain, or is near a known earthquake fault line. If so, this type of coverage will be quite expensive, possibly at a level that is unaffordable.

> **Tip:** Verify with your agent that your insurance coverage takes effect as soon as you take ownership of a property. Even a gap of a few hours presents the risk of uninsured damage.

> **Tip:** Set up a calendar event to update your insurance coverage once a year. It is especially important to adjust the coverage to match any changes in the value of your property.

> **Tip:** Require your tenants to obtain renter's insurance, which covers any losses on their belongings or damage caused by their negligence. You will also benefit, because it covers any claims that may arise from a tenant triggering a fire or causing water damage. Also, tenants are more likely to make claims against this policy, rather than make claims against your policy.

If you own multiple properties, you might be able to get a price discount by purchasing a single policy that covers all of the properties.

Payment Processing

There are some issues with accepting cash from tenants. Though you may accept it occasionally, it is better to use some alternative form of payment, such as a check, in order to mitigate the risk of theft. In addition, if you employ someone who collects rent payments, then there is a risk of theft by this person when payments are made in cash.

Accepting check payments is common, but consider having a policy for dealing with checks that bounce due to insufficient funds in a tenant's bank account. You should pass through to the tenant the not-sufficient-funds fee that the bank will charge you. In addition, consider mandating payments with a cashier's check or money order for a few months thereafter, to ensure that you are actually receiving the required payments.

> **Tip:** Acquire a check scanner from your bank, so that you can scan checks directly into your bank account. Doing so eliminates trips to the bank, and gives you quicker notice of any checks that will not clear the bank. Many banks offer apps that allow you to make a deposit simply by taking a picture of the front and back of a check with your smartphone.

Maintain a Security Deposits Bank Account

Many states require that you store the funds from all tenant security deposits in a separate bank account, and may even require you to notify tenants of the location of this account. Even if these requirements are not in place, it is a good idea to segregate security deposit funds. Otherwise, if you commingle these funds with your other cash, it is quite possible that you will not have the cash available when a tenant eventually moves out and demands repayment of the deposit.

> **Tip:** Prepare and regularly update a supporting schedule that itemizes the exact contents of the bank account in which you store tenant security deposits. The balance in the account (and the schedule) will change over time, as tenants come and go.

Use Anonymized Key Storage

All unit keys should be stored in a locked key safe. In addition, identify each key with an anonymized code, so that an intruder will not know which key is associated with which unit. This is much better than tagging each key with the address of the specific unit.

> **Tip:** Do not use a master key system where a single key provides access to all of your units, because the loss of this key will require you to re-key every unit.

Summary

If you are tightly organized, it is much easier to manage several rental properties. While the number of organizational issues in this chapter might initially seem overwhelming, implementing them one-by-one over a period of months will convert what may be a chaotic situation into one that can be readily overseen with a certain degree of equanimity.

Glossary

I

Income statement. A report that shows the revenues, expenses, and the resulting profits or losses of a business for a specific period of time.

L

Landlord. A person who rents an apartment or a building to a tenant.

Lease. A contract under which a lessor conveys a property to a lessee for a fixed period of time in exchange for compensation.

P

Preventive maintenance. Maintenance that is regularly and routinely performed on assets to reduce the chance of equipment failure.

S

Security deposit. A returnable sum, payable when something is rented, to cover any possible loss or damage.

T

Tenant. A person who occupies property rented from a landlord.

W

Wear and tear. The amount of damage that comes from ordinary use.

Index

www.ingramcontent.com/pod-product-compliance
Lightning Source LLC
Chambersburg PA
CBHW080721220326
41520CB00056B/7343